Happy Holidays!

Kwanzaa

by Betsy Rathburn

BELLWETHER MEDIA
MINNEAPOLIS, MN

BLASTOFF!
Beginners

Blastoff! Beginners are developed by literacy experts and educators to meet the needs of early readers. These engaging informational texts support young children as they begin reading about their world. Through simple language and high frequency words paired with crisp, colorful photos, Blastoff! Beginners launch young readers into the universe of independent reading.

Blastoff! Universe ★

Reading Level — Grade K

Grades 1-3

Grade 4

Sight Words in This Book 🔍

a	each	have	on	their
an	eat	here	other	they
and	for	in	people	time
black	get	is	red	too
day	has	it	the	up

This edition first published in 2023 by Bellwether Media, Inc.

No part of this publication may be reproduced in whole or in part without written permission of the publisher. For information regarding permission, write to Bellwether Media, Inc., Attention: Permissions Department, 6012 Blue Circle Drive, Minnetonka, MN 55343.

Library of Congress Cataloging-in-Publication Data

Names: Rathburn, Betsy, author.
Title: Kwanzaa / by Betsy Rathburn.
Description: Minneapolis, MN : Bellwether Media, 2023. | Series: Happy holidays! | Includes bibliographical references and index. | Audience: Ages 4-7 | Audience: Grades K-1
Identifiers: LCCN 2022009295 (print) | LCCN 2022009296 (ebook) | ISBN 9781644876817 (library binding) | ISBN 9781648348570 (paperback) | ISBN 9781648347276 (ebook)
Subjects: LCSH: Kwanzaa--Juvenile literature. | African Americans--Social life and customs--Juvenile literature.
Classification: LCC GT4403 .R37 2023 (print) | LCC GT4403 (ebook) | DDC 394.2612--dc23/eng/20220224
LC record available at https://lccn.loc.gov/2022009295
LC ebook record available at https://lccn.loc.gov/2022009296

Text copyright © 2023 by Bellwether Media, Inc. BLASTOFF! BEGINNERS and associated logos are trademarks and/or registered trademarks of Bellwether Media, Inc.

Editor: Christina Leaf   Designer: Laura Sowers

Printed in the United States of America, North Mankato, MN.

Table of Contents

It Is Kwanzaa!

A family lights black, red, and green candles. Kwanzaa is here!

candles

A Time for Family

Kwanzaa starts
on December 26.

It lasts
seven days.
Each day has
a **value**.

It is an
African American
holiday.
Other people
join in, too.

It is a time for family. People honor their **roots**.

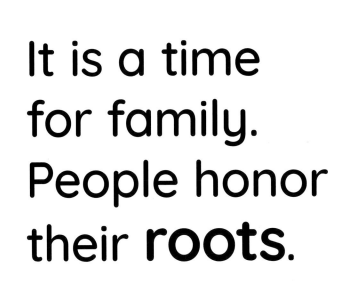

Candles for Kwanzaa

People get a table ready. They set up seven special things.

They light a candle each day. Each candle means something.

People have
a **feast**.
They eat
special foods.

feast

People give gifts
on the last day.
Happy Kwanzaa!

gift

Kwanzaa Facts

Celebrating Kwanzaa

family

candles

gifts

Kwanzaa Activities

light candles

have a feast

give gifts

Glossary

feast

a large meal in honor of something

roots

a person's background or history

value

a belief that is important to someone

To Learn More

ON THE WEB

FACTSURFER

Factsurfer.com gives you
a safe, fun way to find
more information.

1. Go to www.factsurfer.com.

2. Enter "Kwanzaa" into the search box
   and click 🔍.

3. Select your book cover to see a list
   of related content.

Index

The images in this book are reproduced through the courtesy of: Ailisa, front cover, p. 16; Zepherwind, p. 3; Inti St. Clair/ Getty, pp. 4-5; Lisa5201, pp. 6-7; Burke/ Triolo Productions/ Getty, pp. 8-9; David Cooper/ Contributor/ Getty, pp. 10-11; Hill Street Studios/ Getty, pp. 12-13, 20-21; Kayte Deioma/ Alamy, p. 14; Cultura Creative RF/ Alamy, pp. 14-15; Alexander Mychko/ Alamy, p. 18; Miami Herald/ Contributor/ Getty, pp. 18-19, 23 (feast); Quang Ho, p. 20; Yellow Dog Productions/ Getty, p. 22; ZUMA Press, Inc./ Alamy, p. 22 (light candles); Associated Press/ AP Images, pp. 22 (have a feast), 23 (roots); Photo Network/ Alamy, p. 22 (give gifts); Monkey Business Images, p. 23 (value).